THE CIVIL WAR

WAR

BY JIM OLLHOFF

VISIT US AT
WWW.ABDOPUBLISHING.COM

Published by ABDO Publishing Company, 8000 West 78th Street, Suite 310, Edina, MN 55439. Copyright ©2011 by Abdo Consulting Group, Inc. International copyrights reserved in all countries. No part of this book may be reproduced in any form without written permission from the publisher. ABDO & Daughters™ is a trademark and logo of ABDO Publishing Company.

Printed in the United States of America, North Mankato, Minnesota.
112010
012011

♺ PRINTED ON RECYCLED PAPER

Editor: John Hamilton
Graphic Design: John Hamilton
Cover Design: Neil Klinepier
Cover Photo: Getty Images
Interior Photos and Illustrations: Corbis-pgs 10-11, 28-29; Getty Images-pg 17; Granger Collection-pgs 4, 5, 6-7, 8, 9, 12-13, 15, 16, 18, 19, 20, 21, 24, 26-27; John Hamilton-pgs 22-23, 25; ThinkStock-pg 14.

Library of Congress Cataloging-in-Publication Data

Ollhoff, Jim, 1959-
  The Civil War / Jim Ollhoff.
    p. cm. -- (African-American history)
  Includes index.
  ISBN 978-1-61714-710-4
  1. United States--History--Civil War, 1861-1865--Juvenile literature. I. Title. II. Series.

E468.O55 2011
973.7--dc22

                              2010038381

CONTENTS

COLLISION COURSE

From the early 1500s to the 1800s, about 12 million Africans were kidnapped and sold as slaves in North and South America. The slave trade was cruel and horrible, ripping families apart and selling human beings like property.

Slave owners believed that Africans were inferior, and so it was okay to enslave them. Slaves worked in cotton, rice, and tobacco fields, from sunrise to sunset. It was brutal and backbreaking work. They were constantly shackled, and frequently whipped and beaten.

People who wanted to end slavery were called abolitionists. The abolitionists held conferences, wrote articles and books, and tried to stop slavery in the courts.

Slave owners wanted to continue using slaves, and their voices grew louder. The abolitionists argued back. The two sides were on a collision course, and that collision was called the American Civil War.

Slaves cutting and loading sugar cane on a plantation in the American South. Plantation owners who raised crops such as sugar cane, cotton, and tobacco often used cheap slave labor to maximize their profits.

Jack, an African-born slave from today's Republic of Guinea, owned by the B.F. Taylor plantation near Columbia, South Carolina, 1850.

FREE STATES
SLAVE STATES

Southern states had large farms called plantations. They grew cotton, tobacco, and other crops. These crops needed a lot of care and support. Slave owners believed that the only way they could make a profit was through the use of slave labor.

Northern states were more industrial. They had more manufacturing facilities and factories. The Northern states didn't need slaves, and so they grew increasingly anti-slavery. However, many Northerners were still afraid that large numbers of blacks would come north and take their jobs and increase competition in their businesses.

Beginning in the late 1700s, tensions grew between slave states and free states. States each sent representatives to the United States Congress to make legislation. Both the slave states and the free states wanted more votes than the other, in order to pass laws that benefited them. They negotiated, debated, and compromised, and so kept the number of slave states and free states even. Every new state became a battleground—should it be a free or slave state?

After the sale: a scene from a slave market of the mid-1800s in Richmond, Virginia.

One by one, beginning in the 1780s, the Northern states made slavery illegal. In 1808, importing slaves became illegal in the United States. However, the law was only enforced in the Northern states.

In 1820, there were 11 free states and 11 slave states. Missouri and Maine were asking for statehood. The debate about slavery was the central issue for Missouri. Finally, a law was proposed called the Missouri Compromise. It said Maine would be a free state and Missouri would be a slave state. The bill also said that slavery would be illegal in the rest of the territories of the Midwest, north of Missouri.

In the years 1846–1848, Mexico and the United States fought a war over control of a huge area of the Southwest. The United States won the war. It took over land in the present-day states of Texas, Arizona, New Mexico, and California. This war was followed by more controversy. Should the new areas allow slavery or not?

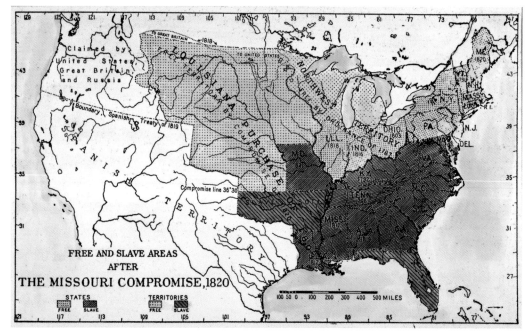

A map of the United States showing the free and slave states and territories following the Missouri Compromise of 1820.

Bleeding Kansas: The sacking of Lawrence, Kansas, by pro-slavery forces on May 21, 1856. Kansas was eventually admitted as a free state.

G.H.HAYES sc

In 1854, Kansas requested admission to statehood in the United States. This created a huge debate over whether it should be admitted as a free state or slave state. A number of conventions, rallies, and protests were held in Kansas. As tempers flared, many of the protests became violent. East Coast newspapers referred to the territory as Bleeding Kansas. Kansas was eventually admitted as a free state.

Senators and representatives of the United States Congress tried to keep the country intact. Despite a growing feeling that slavery was morally wrong, leaders worked on compromises to keep the union of states from drifting further apart.

PUSHING FOR FREEDOM

Slavery was horrible, but several events made it seem like freedom might come soon. In 1772, under pressure from the church, slavery became illegal in England. This didn't apply to England's colonies in North America. However, it was a sign of hope.

In 1776, Thomas Jefferson wrote the Declaration of Independence, declaring that the United States was no longer under England's control. Jefferson wrote the famous words, "All men are created equal." At the time Jefferson wrote this, he himself owned more than 200 slaves.

The Declaration of Independence didn't apply to African Americans. However, the idea was powerful. When anti-slavery forces spoke and wrote, they often used Jefferson's language of equality to attack slavery.

In 1791, there was a violent slave uprising in Haiti. The slave revolt was successful, and slavery was abolished in Haiti. This gave hope to slaves in the United States. However, it also made slave owners more fearful, and they used harsher punishments and were very diligent about preventing slave revolts.

A view inside the dome of the Jefferson Memorial, in Washington, DC. Even though Thomas Jefferson was a slave owner, the words he wrote for the Declaration of Independence—"All men are created equal"—were often used to attack the institution of slavery.

Early in the 1800s, the American Colonization Society began. It was a movement to send Africans back to Africa. The membership of the American Colonization Society was a strange mix. There were many anti-slavery people, who believed that blacks would never be treated fairly in this country. There were racist whites, who were fearful of free blacks in the United States. There were also blacks, who thought that living in Africa would be better than living in the United States. Thousands of blacks got on ships headed for Liberia and Sierra Leone, Africa. As time went on, the American Colonization Society was rejected by the anti-slavery movement.

In 1830, the National Negro Convention began. It was a yearly meeting for blacks to make plans for freedom. They organized boycotts of slave-produced goods. Having an organization that represented them gave blacks a voice. The first convention was chaired by Richard Allen, the founder of the African Methodist Episcopal Church.

Other churches also gave hope to black slaves. In a series of religious revivals called The Great Awakening, preachers traveled the countryside and preached to whomever listened. The preachers gave powerful messages of hope, justice, and freedom. African slaves and poor whites anxiously sought out the messages that God would rescue them.

Abolitionist Wendell Phillips speaking against slavery to a group assembled on Boston Common, Boston, Massachusetts, in 1851.

CONTINUED SLAVERY

Just as there were forces that gave hope to slaves, there were also forces to keep slavery going. The biggest thing that kept slavery going was money. Slave owners made huge profits from their crops. Slave owners made themselves rich because of the cheap labor.

In 1793, Eli Whitney patented his cotton engine (or "cotton gin" for short). It was a machine that filtered out the seeds from the fiber of the cotton. Previously, this was a very time-consuming chore that was done by hand. With the cotton gin, two people could do the work of 100. Cotton plantations expanded, and the southern United States became the world's leading supplier of cotton. As the cotton industry grew, so did the desire for more slaves.

Racist ideas and attitudes continued to spread. For example, cartoons in newspapers often pictured African Americans as being inferior to white people. And songs like "Jump Jim Crow" in 1828 mocked African American culture.

James Forten encouraged African Americans to stay in this country and fight for their freedom.

James Forten (1766–1842)

Born in Philadelphia, Pennsylvania, Forten was an inventor and a powerful speaker against slavery. His early schooling was at an all-black school run by Quakers. His inventions included sailing tools for ships.

Forten spoke out against the American Colonization Society, which wanted to send blacks back to Africa. He said that blacks must stay in the land that had been enriched with their blood and sweat. He encouraged blacks to stay and fight for freedom.

This print shows Frederick Douglass speaking while a Boston, Massachusetts, mob and police break up an abolitionist meeting in Tremont Temple, December 3, 1860.

Frederick Douglass (1818?–1895)

Born as a slave in Maryland, Frederick Douglass lost his parents at an early age. He learned to read and write, and became a great speaker. He spoke so thoughtfully and powerfully that he was in great demand at anti-slavery rallies. The autobiography of his life as a slave became an international bestseller. He consulted with President Abraham Lincoln and became one of the foremost opponents of slavery.

Frederick Douglass

MARCHING TOWARD WAR

The passions for and against slavery continued to boil. In the years before the Civil War, the passions often boiled over into riots. In 1852, Harriet Beecher

Stowe

Stowe wrote a book called *Uncle Tom's Cabin*. It was a novel that depicted the horrors of slavery, as well as the power of love. It became the best-selling novel in the 1800s. Its powerful anti-slavery message gave tremendous fuel for anti-slavery activists.

"The Death of Uncle Tom," from a 19th-century edition of Harriet Beecher Stowe's *Uncle Tom's Cabin*.

Protesters watch as federal and state troops return Anthony Burns to slavery after his trial in Boston, Massachusetts.

In 1854, in Boston, Massachusetts, an escaped slave named Anthony Burns was arrested by bounty hunters, and locked up in jail. Conventions and rallies followed for several days. Finally, a mob of protesters tried to rescue Burns from jail. President Franklin Pierce called the U.S. Marines to Boston. Anti-slavery publisher William Lloyd Garrison burned a copy of the United States Constitution, saying it was "a covenant with death and an agreement with hell." Protesters hung coffins in the streets. Burns eventually was sent back to the South, where supporters bought his freedom. However, the events showed the deep divisions that ran through the country.

Dred Scott (1799?–1858)

In 1857, another event inflamed passions across the United States. A Missouri slave named Dred Scott sued his owner, saying that he should be set free. The case went all the way to the United States Supreme Court. The court said that blacks were not citizens of the United States and not protected by the Constitution. It was clearly a decision based in racism, and it powerfully inflamed anti-slavery activists. Many people on both sides of the issue began to believe that the slavery issue would eventually come to violence.

In 1859, a white abolitionist named John Brown gathered some whites and blacks and raided a weapons arsenal at Harpers Ferry, Virginia (in today's West Virginia). They wanted to steal guns and ammunition to start a slave revolt. The raid was defeated by troops under the command of Robert E. Lee, who would later command the Confederate forces during the Civil War. John Brown was captured and hanged. To Southern slave owners, John Brown was a criminal and a traitor. But to Northern anti-slavery activists, he was a hero who died for a noble cause.

Inside the Harpers Ferry Armory, where John Brown and his men were trapped by U.S. Marines.

William Lloyd Garrison (1805–1879)

A newspaper editor, journalist, and speaker for women's rights,

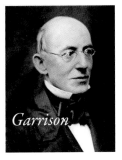

Garrison

William Lloyd Garrison was one of the foremost activists against slavery. At an early age, he began to speak out for emancipation, the act of letting slaves go free. He created his own anti-slavery newspaper, the *Liberator*. He was attacked by mobs, threatened with hanging, and dragged through the streets, but his fiery anger about slavery never stopped. At Garrison's funeral, Frederick Douglass said, "It was the glory of this man that he could stand alone with the truth, and calmly await the result."

THE AMERICAN CIVIL WAR

There were many issues that divided the Northern states and the Southern states. The Northern states were more industrial, and more based in cities. The Southern states were more based in agriculture, and had many huge plantations. The Northern and Southern states resented each other's push for more power in the government. Each side felt that its own way of life would be destroyed if the other side gained more political power and influence. Fights over the rights of the states fiercely divided the North and South.

Cannons fire at a Civil War reenactment in Boscobel, Wisconsin.

But of all the issues separating the North and South, no issue inflamed more passion than slavery. When Abraham Lincoln was elected in 1860, the South feared that he would end slavery. Several Southern states had already seceded, or separated, from the Union by the time Lincoln took office. The frantic attempts to compromise and negotiate failed.

In 1861, Southern forces attacked Fort Sumter in Charleston, South Carolina. Abraham Lincoln immediately called for an army to keep the nation of states intact. Since the army would have to march through Virginia and North Carolina, those states quickly joined the Confederate States of America. The American Civil War had begun.

The 54th Massachusetts Volunteer Infantry Regiment storming Fort Wagner, South Carolina, on July 18, 1863. The regiment was one of the first army units made up mainly of African American troops.

At first, blacks were not allowed to fight for the Union. President Abraham Lincoln was mostly interested in preserving the union of states. He was afraid that if African American soldiers were allowed to fight, it would seem like the war was a slave revolt, instead of a war to preserve the United States. However, after some early Union defeats on the battlefield, Lincoln changed his mind. Frederick Douglass encouraged the president to allow African Americans to fight for their freedom.

The United States created a part of the army called the Colored Troops, which contained only black soldiers. They fought bravely through the war, and were involved in more than 400 battles. Blacks also served as spies behind Confederate lines, because they could pretend to be Southern slaves.

There were about 180,000 black soldiers in the Union Army— almost 10 percent of the total. The Confederacy promised freedom for blacks who joined the Confederate forces, but only a few did so.

Reenactor Ricky Townsell portraying a member of Wisconsin's Company F, 29th Infantry Regiment, U.S.C.T.

THE EMANCIPATION PROCLAMATION

On January 1, 1863, President Abraham Lincoln issued an executive order known as the Emancipation Proclamation. It freed slaves in states that were not under federal control. This first executive order didn't make slavery illegal. It was a symbolic gesture, but also a tool to try to undermine the Confederacy. The border states that were loyal to the Union soon did away with slavery. The anti-slavery forces were moving fast and furiously. This proclamation also created a new goal for the Union forces: to free the slaves.

Supporters of Lincoln's executive order were concerned that it only freed the slaves, but didn't make slavery illegal. So, in January 1865, a law was proposed by Congress. It was the Thirteenth Amendment to the Constitution of the United States. The amendment made slavery illegal.

The Civil War ended in April 1865, when Confederate General Robert E. Lee surrendered. Five days after the surrender, a Confederate activist named John Wilkes Booth shot and killed Abraham Lincoln.

President Abraham Lincoln reading the Emancipation Proclamation to his cabinet in Washington, DC.

RACISM
CONTINUES

The war was over, and the world had changed. Black slaves were free, but the Southern states had been destroyed by war. Cities lay in ruins. The economy was in shambles. Before he died, Abraham Lincoln had already put together a plan for reconstructing the South.

However, reconstruction didn't go as planned, because Lincoln had been assassinated. Vice President Andrew Johnson took over. He was a former slave owner, and sympathetic to the Southern states.

Even though slavery was over, several Southern states created racist laws to keep black Americans from achieving full equality. Some laws restricted where African Americans could live. Other laws prohibited blacks from testifying against whites in court. Some laws tried to regulate where African Americans could work.

Even after the Civil War, there was continued inequality and segregation. In the years ahead, African Americans and whites fought for equality. It would take remarkable courage by many Americans to create continued freedom and progress toward equal rights.

Three young African American boys huddle against a pillar in the ruins of Charleston, South Carolina.

GLOSSARY

ABOLITIONIST

An activist who fought for freedom for slaves.

CIVIL WAR

The war fought between America's Northern and Southern states from 1861–1865. The Southern states were for slavery. They wanted to start their own country. Northern states fought against slavery and a division of the country.

CONFEDERACY

The Southern states of Alabama, Arkansas, Florida, Georgia, Louisiana, Mississippi, North Carolina, South Carolina, Tennessee, Texas, and Virginia. These states wanted to keep slavery legal. They broke away from the United States during the Civil War and formed their own country known as the Confederate States of America, or the Confederacy. The Confederacy ended in 1865 when the war ended and the 11 Confederate states rejoined the United States.

CONSTITUTION

A set of laws that establish the rules and principles of a country or organization.

COTTON GIN

A machine invented by Eli Whitney to remove seeds from cotton fibers, a job previously done by hand that was very time consuming.

Emancipation

To be set free. For many African Americans, emancipation after the Civil War meant freedom from slavery.

Great Awakening

A Christian revival, where preachers traveled through the countryside and preached to whomever who listen.

Plantation

A very large farm common in the South, usually growing crops such as cotton, rice, or tobacco. To make the plantations more profitable, owners often relied on cheap slave labor.

Racism

The belief that people of one skin color are better than a people of another skin color, or that individuals of a certain skin color have certain characteristics *because* of their skin color.

Secede

To withdraw from a membership or alliance. During the Civil War, a group of 11 states seceded from the United States to form the Confederate States of America.

Segregation

The separation of people based on the color of their skin.

Union

Another name for the United States, especially during the Civil War.

INDEX